AF579064

For Fizza, Hakim, Zehra and Zarina

Published in 1996 by:
HSP Publications
Head office: 7 Highgate High Street, Highgate Village,
London N6 5JR
Also: P.O.Box 3181,170 Gizenga Street, Zanzibar

Photographs by Javed Jafferji
Introduction and captions by Bethan Rees Jones

Illustrations: Muzu Sulemanji
Design: Nick Ballantine Associates
Colour Origination: Columbia Offset
Printers: Tien Wah Press

ACKNOWLEDGMENTS

We would like to thank the following people for their help and kindness during the making of this book: Walid Fikirini, Captain Peter Hendricks, Raymond Chemah, Hassan Hirji, Gillian Lyons, Matt Richmond, Mark Thomas and the staff of 'The Gallery Zanzibar'

Photographs used in this books are available for commercial use from:
Impact Photos, 26-27 Great Sutton Street,
London EC1V ODX

ISBN No 0-9521726-4-X

British Library Cataloguing-in-Publication Data
A Catalogue record for this book is available from the British Library

IMAGES • OF
ZANZIBAR

Photographs by JAVED JAFFERJI

Introduction by BETHAN REES JONES

Published by HSP Publications
First edition1996

INTRODUCTION

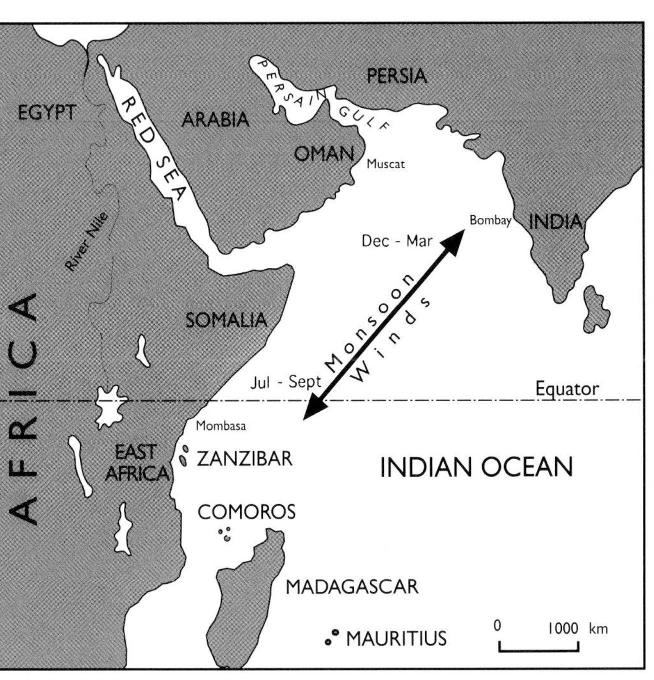

Zanzibar: between Africa and the Indian Ocean. The monsoon winds connected Zanzibar with the Orient, which was important for its trade and its history.

Zanzibar. The name conjures up images of slaves, spices and sultans but is as elusive as the labyrinth of narrow streets which twist and turn through the Stone Town. Everyone has heard of Zanzibar, yet no one is quite sure exactly where it is. In fact, Zanzibar refers to two Indian Ocean islands, Zanzibar, known in Kiswahili as Unguja, six degrees south of the equator and Pemba, 50 km to the north-east. Between the islands lies the Pemba Channel, famous for its deep waters which harbour a variety of marine life. Coral reefs are scattered around the islands and the colour of the sea lightens to aquamarine in their vicinity. The islands have different geological formations and Zanzibar is as flat as Pemba is hilly, with emerald rice paddies in the steep valleys. Pemba is fringed by mangroves in inlets around the coast and from the air, rivers can be seen fanning out to sea in the tidal estuaries. Famous for their spices, the islands are an exotic mixture where Africa merges with the Orient in the shape of the Swahili people and their culture.

For thousands of years, *dhows* similar to those which anchor in the harbour today, sailed down the African coast from the Arabian peninsula on the north-east monsoon or *kaskazi*. They carried salted fish, beads, cloth and Chinese porcelain which was used to decorate mosques, tombs and houses. At this period, from December to March, the weather is hot and dry and the sailors would wait for *masika* or the heavy rains to pass before sailing north on the southerly monsoon, *kusi*, which is strongest from July to September. They took back food grains, mangrove poles, spices, slaves, tortoiseshell, ebony, ivory and gold. Hippalus, an Egyptian, wrote about the existence of the monsoon winds in the first century BC, thus letting the Western world in on a secret kept by the Arabs and Indians for centuries.

THE STONE TOWN

Approaching Unguja from the sea, the first sighting of the island is a blur of green sitting low on the horizon. Passing sand banks fringed by turquoise water, individual palm trees can gradually be made out, fronds rippling in the breeze. Zanzibar Town sits on a triangular peninsula, on the west coast of the island. Originally the site of a fishing village, local legend tells that Hassan, the *Mwinyi Mkuu* (great leader), decreed in 1725 that the bush should be cleared for a larger settlement to be built, which became the site of the modern city.

Sailing around the point of the peninsula into the harbour, stately, crenellated houses come into view along the sea front. White walls support corrugated iron roofs, rusted to the colour of beaten earth; the skyline is pierced by a tall minaret and the silver spires of a church. In spite of its medieval atmosphere, most of the stone buildings of the town date from the nineteenth century. The architectural form is largely Omani Arab but it is influenced by the blending of African, Indian and European cultures. The Stone Town houses are built of coral rocks cemented together with a mixture of lime, clay and sand, with mangrove poles used as beams to support roofs and ceilings.

It became a matter of status to live in the Stone Town. Houses were often built around a central courtyard, with flat roofs which were edged by a crenellated wall on wealthier mansions. The buildings were usually austere in form, possibly due to the influence of the Ibadhis, a purist Islamic sect. Decorative detail was often focused on the intricately carved doorways and over five hundred examples can be seen in Zanzibar town. It was the custom to order a carved door-frame first and then when it had been fixed in place, to build the house on to it. Some doors were imported from India, others carved locally from jack fruit tree or imported teak. The date was often carved on the lintel together with the householder's monogram - an important indication of social status. In the mid-nineteenth century, Richard Burton, the explorer noted that:

> *.....the higher the tenement, the bigger the gateway, the heavier the padlock and the huger the iron studs that nail the door of heavy timber, the greater is the owner's dignity.*

Arab doors were usually set into a square frame and the carving often incorporated fish, chain and lotus motifs; Indian doors had arched tops and the carving was often more elaborate, with baroque floral patterns. Some doors were adorned with brass studs which may be a decorative adaptation of the Indian custom of fortifying doors against the attack of war elephants. The carved symbols are thought to represent fertility, wealth, security and plenty and together with a quotation from the Koran they offered the householder protection for himself and his family.

Along the houses, you find the *baraza*, a low stone bench built on

either side of the narrow streets. Here men in particular sit and talk outside their homes or near the neighbourhood mosque. It forms a significant characteristic of the Stone Town and the *baraza*, which in Kiswahili means 'meeting place', becomes a means of establishing contact with passers-by. Coffee sellers often use them as an outdoor cafe before moving on to the next neighbourhood. The *baraza* has a practical function when the streets are flooded during the rainy season. One of the earliest drainage systems in Africa has gradually been silted up by sand used in the town to wash dishes. During heavy downpours, rainwater flows in murky rivers through the town; to the sea in one direction and to the former site of the creek in the other, turning the market into a floating world. The *barazas* are high enough off the ground to offer shelter from the flooded streets. People wait here for the rain to stop or use them as elevated pavements, stepping from one to another, high above the floodwater.

Wandering through the narrow streets, you pass houses, public buildings, palaces and small gardens which are often the site of tombs. The tall houses cast deep shadows which are a welcome relief from the equatorial sun. Windows are shuttered in the afternoon and then opened later to catch any breeze blowing in from the Indian Ocean. Balconies and verandas provide an extension to the house where the sunlight is filtered by fretwork and latticework screens. The sunlight is softened and in previous years it allowed women in purdah to see outside whilst remaining hidden from passers-by on the street. Some houses had small arched openings in the parapet wall below the roof for the same reason. Adjoining houses and palaces were sometimes linked by a *wikio* or bridge so that women could pass unseen from one to the other without having to walk through the streets.

Historical Background

The name 'Swahili' comes from *sawahil*, the Arabic word for coast and originally Bantu tribes migrated to the area, becoming the 'people of the coast'. The tribes of Zanzibar are the *Wahadimu, Watumbatu* and *Wapemba* and they probably came from the mainland in search of seasonal fishing areas. They formed small village communities with their own chiefs and traditionally lived by subsistence farming with small herds of sheep or goats.

To the Arabs the area was known as *Zinjbar* or 'land of the black men' and the Zinj Empire flourished during the fourteenth century. City

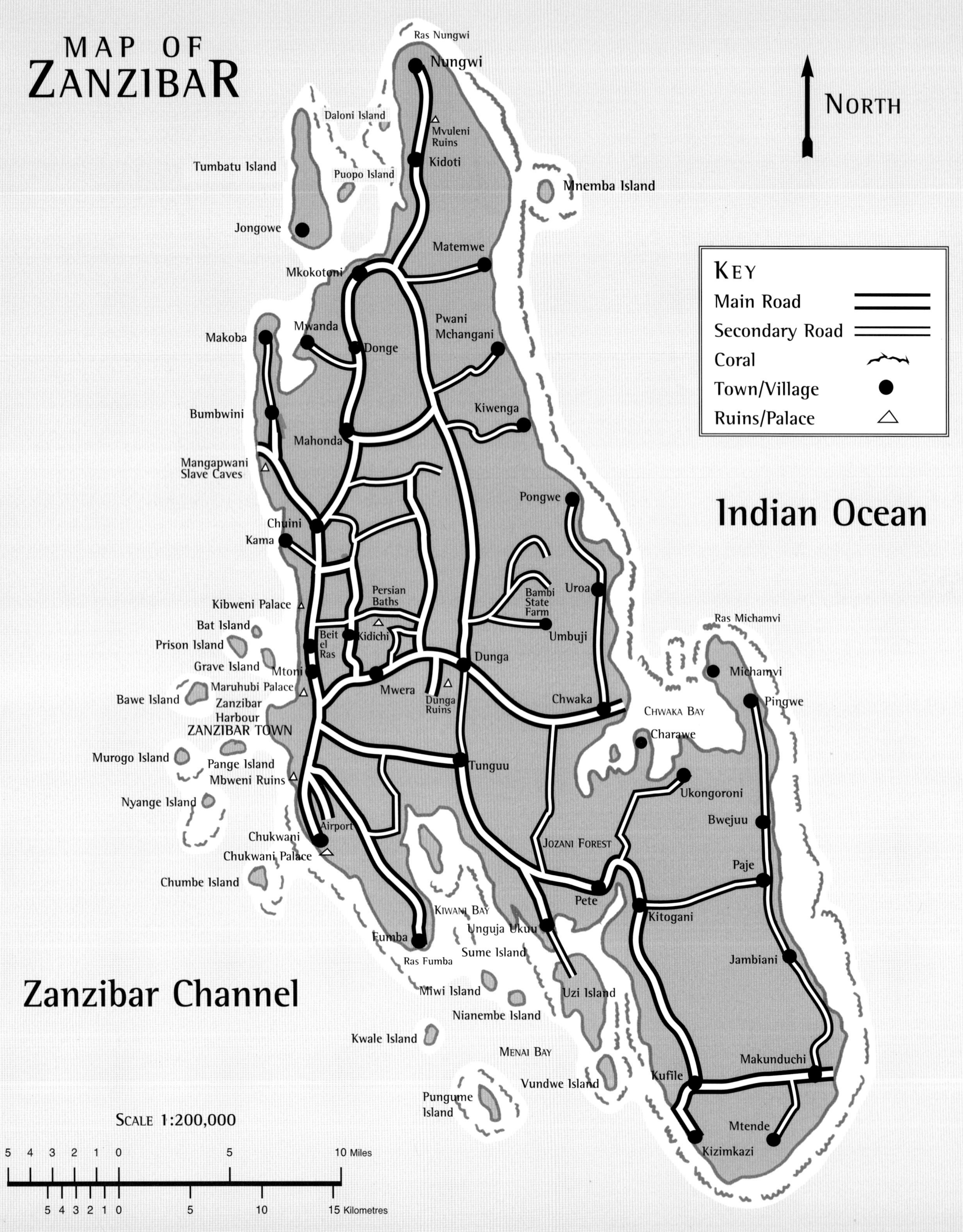
MAP OF ZANZIBAR
NORTH
Ras Nungwi
Nungwi
Daloni Island
Mvuleni Ruins
Tumbatu Island
Puopo Island
Kidoti
Mnemba Island
Jongowe
Matemwe
Mkokotoni
Makoba
Mwanda
Donge
Pwani Mchangani
Bumbwini
Kiwenga
Mahonda
Mangapwani Slave Caves
Pongwe
Chuini
Kama
Indian Ocean
Persian Baths
Kibweni Palace
Bambi State Farm
Uroa
Bat Island
Umbuji
Prison Island
Beit el Ras
Kidichi
Grave Island
Mtoni
Dunga
Maruhubi Palace
Mwera
Bawe Island
Zanzibar Harbour
Dunga Ruins
Chwaka
ZANZIBAR TOWN
Murogo Island
Pange Island
Tunguu
Mbweni Ruins
Nyange Island
Airport
Chukwani
Chukwani Palace
Chumbe Island
Kiwani Bay
Fumba
Ras Fumba
Unguja Ukuu
Sume Island
Zanzibar Channel
Miwi Island
Nianembe Island
Kwale Island
Menai Bay
Pungume Island
Vundwe Island
Uzi Island
Jozani Forest
Pete
Kitogani
Chwaka Bay
Charawe
Ukongoroni
Ras Michamvi
Michamvi
Pingwe
Bwejuu
Paje
Jambiani
Makunduchi
Kufile
Mtende
Kizimkazi
Key
Main Road
Secondary Road
Coral
Town/Village
Ruins/Palace
Scale 1:200,000
5 4 3 2 1 0 5 10 Miles
5 4 3 2 1 0 5 10 15 Kilometres

states were scattered along the East African coast with a literate Muslim culture and a trading network spreading within Africa and across the Indian Ocean, with gold particularly in demand. Ocean trade grew up as a result of the monsoon winds which blow across most of the western Indian Ocean as far south as Madagascar. Centuries before the birth of Christ, the Sumerians and Assyrians sailed down the coast to trade, followed later by Egyptians and Phoenicians. The Persians had a considerable influence on the coastal states as they controlled a powerful empire in the Indian Ocean from 600 BC until the 7th century AD. It is still common for Swahili people to claim Persian or Shirazi ancestry.

The first Europeans to arrive on the East African coast were the Portuguese as they searched for the sea route to India. They quickly overthrew the Zinj Empire and took control of the sea lanes along the coast, however they never attempted to colonise the area, only installing small garrisons and collecting a tribute from the local population. They built a church and a small trading settlement in what is now Zanzibar Town. The period 1500-1700 AD was marked by minor rebellions along the coast and the beginning of the real decline of Portuguese power came in 1622. After driving the Portuguese from Muscat, Arab fleets led by Sultan bin Seif, eliminated their control further and further south. Mombasa and Pemba fell in 1627 and by 1635, Unguja too was freed. There are a few relics of Portuguese influence left on the islands - they introduced new food crops such as cassava and cashew nuts, both originally from Brazil; words such as *nanasi* for pineapple and *meza* for table and the interesting custom of bull-fighting in Pemba. It is known as *mchezo wa ngombe*, 'the game of the bull' and it is a harmless variation of the sport as the bull is not hurt. People traditionally believed that the ritual fight helped to bring the rain needed before planting crops and it is usually held after the clove harvest as a means of celebration.

The Omani Arabs now stepped in to take control of the coast but they also encountered some resistance from the Swahili. During the eighteenth century, the Arabs built a fort on the site of the Portuguese Church in Zanzibar Town. They used Unguja as a watering and provisioning centre and by 1729, they controlled the coast as far south as Mozambique. By now Oman was an important trading nation but the country lacked the manpower to work on its date plantations. As Islam forbade the enslavement of Muslims, African slaves were used to provide the necessary labour and many began to be transported through Unguja. By the end of the eighteenth century, Swahili and Arab traders headed caravans into the interior. Unguja's position as a trade centre increased when ivory began to be shipped through the island to avoid the high Portuguese export duties in Mozambique.

For the next few years, Oman was troubled by dynastic disputes and invasion by the Persians. After settling these problems, Sultan Seyyid Said set sail in 1828 to subdue an uprising in Mombasa. He continued down the coast to Unguja and recognised the island's importance as a base from which to control trade, both along the coast and with the interior of Africa. The island had safe harbours and a fresh water supply to attract passing ships as well as fertile agricultural land. Perhaps because it was also at a safe distance from potential rivals in Oman, Seyyid Said moved his capital to Unguja in 1832, although the *Mwinyi Mkuu,* Hassan II was still permitted to preside over local matters.

This marked a profound change in the history of the islands. The Omani Arabs introduced clove trees and found they did well in the hot, damp climate. They began to clear and cultivate the forested western part of Unguja, where the fertile, red soil known as *changa* clay is thickest. Only pockets of primeval forest, such as Jozani remained. Fertile soils are more widespread in Pemba and the island became known in Arabic as *al Khudra*, the green island, the richest agricultural region in East Africa. Sultan Seyyid Said realized that production was an important step to develop the islands instead of relying on trade alone and he therefore issued a decree stating that every plantation owner had to plant three clove trees for every coconut palm or forfeit his estate. The islands' prosperity increased, as did the demand for slaves to work on the plantations. By the middle of the nineteenth century, two-thirds of the islands' population were slaves and thousands were exported annually to Arabia, Persia and other eastern countries.

Many Arabs followed the Sultan, realising that Oman's prosperity was in decline, while Unguja was now the centre of the trade in slaves, ivory and firearms. Powers in the northern hemisphere wanted to share in this trade and the US was the first country to open a consulate in 1833, followed by Britain in 1841 and soon after by France, Portugal, Italy, Belgium and Germany. Zanzibar Town became the starting point for journeys into the interior for missionaries and explorers and the place where they equipped their expeditions with porters and supplies. Richard Burton and David Livingstone paid their respects to the Sultan, who was by now the nominal ruler of an empire stretching from Mozambique as far north as Turkana and west into Malawi, Zambia and Zaire and whose lands they would be passing through.

On Seyyid Said's death in 1856, his second surviving son, Seyyid Majid, succeeded to the throne in Zanzibar and his East African possessions. Four years later Zanzibar became an independent sultanate, separate from the sultanate in Oman. Majid's reign was uneventful apart from an unsuccessful attempt by his brother Barghash to seize the throne. After a period of exile in India, Barghash became sultan in 1870 and during his eighteen year reign, Zanzibar became world-famous. Perhaps influenced by the riches of India, he adopted a more elaborate style of living than the former sultans and erected several new palaces. In the town, he built Beit el-Ajaib, the House of Wonders, for ceremonial purposes. It was the largest building ever seen in Zanzibar and the first to have electric light. It contained beautiful examples of carved doors inscribed in gilt with text from the Koran, marble pavements, silver decorations on the staircases as well as an electric lift.

Out of town he built palaces at Chuini, Chukwani, Migombani and Marahubi. For the latter, he bought the estate from an Arab of the Marahubi tribe in the 1880s. At the end of an avenue of mango trees, a palace, Persian baths and artificial ponds filled with water lilies were built for the use of his harem. For the baths, stone aqueducts were constructed to supply water from Chem Chem, a natural spring which was believed to have miraculous powers. In the past, people would go to pray and sacrifice animals at its edge. The palace was accidentally burnt down in 1899 and only the pillars which supported the balconies, a few crumbling walls and the baths now remain. The area is still thickly planted with mango trees and some people prefer to avoid the area at night as *pepo* spirits are said to perch in the trees waiting to drop down onto an unsuspecting victim and to possess them by sitting on their heads.

Sultan Barghash did not only look after his own comfort but he instigated several projects to improve the amenities of the Stone Town. A police force was set up and a street lighting system introduced which improved the safety of the public, particularly during the north-east monsoon when the town was filled with slave traders and pirates. He also had a covered conduit built to bring pure drinking water to the town as many wells had become polluted and attacks of cholera were common. He linked Zanzibar to the outside world by giving the small island of Bawe to the Eastern Telegraph Company to land their cable from Aden.

Throughout his reign, Barghash came under mounting pressure from the British to suppress the slave trade and in 1873, he signed an edict forbidding the transport of slaves from one part of his dominions to another. The slave market at Mkunazini in the town was closed and the site bought by the Universities Mission in Central Africa (UMCA), who built an Anglican Cathedral with the altar standing exactly on the spot where slaves had been tied to a post. It was still possible to own slaves and one of the first effects of the treaty was to push up prices, and smuggling went on, using small coves around the coast.

The loss of revenue from slave trading hit the economy of the islands and a hurricane destroyed many of the clove plantations, dealing another blow. Zanzibar came increasingly under the influence of the British and by 1890 a power struggle between Germany and Britain for control of East African territory ended with little consultation of the Sultan. Germany took over control of mainland Tanganyika and Britain controlled the remainder of East Africa with Zanzibar becoming a British Protectorate in 1891. The Sultan's possessions were reduced to a strip of the coast seven hundred miles long and ten miles wide on the mainland as well as the islands off the coast. On April 5th, 1897, Sultan Hamoud signed a decree abolishing the legal status of slavery on the islands, although it was possible to keep slave concubines until 1911. At the end of the first year, only approximately two thousand slaves of the fifty or sixty thousand on the islands had claimed their freedom, unwilling to give up their harsh yet secure life for possible starvation.

There were a series of short reigning sultans until 1911, when Sultan Seyyid Khalifa bin Harub succeeded to the throne. He reigned until 1960 and was a respected ruler, although the British effectively controlled the islands. Zanzibar Town had been declared a free port in 1892 and prosperity once again increased. By the 1920s, the city bustled with economic activity and the bazaar streets were lined with craftsmen who produced carved doors and brass-studded chests, gold and silver jewellery, pottery and embroidery.

Away from the Stone Town there were problems. There was a severe shortage of labour on the plantations as many freed slaves refused to work and this necessitated the recruitment of workers from the mainland, to help pick cloves during the harvest. Arabs stopped investing in their plantations and many became increasingly indebted to Indian money-lenders. More and more foodstuffs were imported whereas originally the islands, particularly Pemba, had been largely self-sufficient. The development of the islands was hindered for these reasons and the rule of the Al-Busaidi dynasty in East Africa was ended in January 1964, just after the islands gained independence from the British on December 10th, 1963. In a short but bloody revolution, thousands of Arabs were killed. A socialist government was installed and many educated and skilled people fled the country, leaving a vacuum which was filled by communist countries. On April 24th, 1964, Zanzibar and Tanganyika joined to form the United Republic of Tanzania. The Union Government controls foreign affairs and defence matters but Zanzibar maintains some autonomy, with its own President and House of Representatives.

Zanzibar Today

In 1991/92, the government of the islands began to liberalise the economy and more and more goods became available in the shops. Transport links to the mainland improved and international flights now arrive in Unguja. Tourism is increasingly seen as a way of reviving the economy.

Zanzibar's unspoilt beaches are becoming a popular tourist attraction. The beautiful stretch of white sand that a tourist sees is used by the local communities in many ways. The east coast of Unguja is guarded by a long coral reef off the shore, breaking the force of the waves which can be heard roaring in the distance at low tide, the time when people walk through the shallows scouring the reef for shellfish and octopus. The Swahili were traditionally maritime people and today fishing is still an important industry. There are fishing villages around the coast of the islands. Small, thatched huts are set between the palm trees and *ngalawas*, outrigger canoes, wait for the next tide. Fishing is done with nets, hand-lines, traps and increasingly spear fishing is becoming popular, a method which can quickly affect the balance of a reef by removing the larger fish.

Coconut palms are a feature of tropical islands. As well as their scenic value, they have a practical purpose, especially in Unguja, as every part of the tree and coconuts are used. They are the source of copra and coir as well as providing fuel wood and fronds which are used as roofing material and matting. Women bury coconut husks below the tide line to condition them before using the fibre to make rope. In the sandy areas of the reef flat on the east coast, people cultivate seaweed for export and this has become the main cash crop in many villages. The beach is used as a thoroughfare at low tide and people walk or cycle between villages on the sand. Fishermen spread out their nets on the beach to mend any holes and maintain their boats in the shade of the palm trees.

Subsistence farming is practised in all rural areas of the islands and most urban dwellers have a garden in the *shamba* (countryside) which they go to tend during their free time, often arriving back in town on bicycles laden with produce. Cloves are grown in fertile, deep soil areas, largely found on Pemba, and still provide an important export, with an average annual harvest of five thousand tonnes. They are used as a spice, are smoked in cigarettes in Indonesia and are distilled to produce clove oil. During harvest time, schools may be closed so that the children can help with the picking. After they have been dried and graded, the cloves are stored in godowns at the harbour, waiting to be exported and at this time the air in the Stone Town is full of their spicy aroma. Bananas are another important crop and there are several different varieties, the sweet ones are eaten raw and the green ones are cooked. In other areas, maize, cassava, pulses, sesame, chillies, tomatoes and egg-plants are grown as cash crops, together with a wide variety of spices. Coconuts and mangoes are grown in areas with less rainfall. Sugar was grown extensively until the end of the nineteenth century but now cane is grown only for domestic use.

The coast of East Africa was part of the Islamic world from the eleventh century and ninety-seven percent of the islands' population are Muslims, although there are also Hindus, Christians and a small group of Parsees. A mosque is the focus of every neighbourhood, often blending into the surrounding houses except for the *kibla,* the semicircular alcove which juts out to show the congregation the direction of Mecca. Women are swathed in a black *bui bui* in public but beneath they wear exotic, brightly coloured fabrics. Some prefer to wear *khangas*, a pair of cotton cloths, one worn as a skirt and the other as a veil covering the head. For Muslim men a *kanzu*, a long white robe, is the traditional dress and this is worn particularly on Fridays, the Muslim holy day. *Kofia*, beautifully embroidered hats are also associated with Islam.

The *muezzin's* call to prayer echoes across the rooftops five times a day and in between prayers, children can be heard chanting the Koran at the *madrasa* or Koran school. The biggest festival on the islands is Idd el- Fitr, the celebration after Ramadhan, the month of fasting. People exchange presents and new outfits are bought for the entire family. Festival grounds are set up with different booths and stalls offering local food, games, *ngoma* - traditional dances and plays as entertainment. This is also the time to go to a *Taarab* concert, a distinctive style of music on the islands, particularly popular with women. Islam may be translated as 'submission to the will of God and obedience to his laws' and in Zanzibar it is impossible to say 'see you tomorrow', without someone adding, *In'shallah* - 'if God wills it'.

Today the islands hang in the balance, as traditional culture comes up against Western influences. The Stone Town is often busy with tourists searching for curios in the dusty antique shops. Sun-worshippers seek out the perfect beach, deserted apart from the ghost crabs which peep from their burrows. In the villages around the coast, life carries on as it has done for centuries. People rise with the sun and begin their daily tasks, sweeping the house or preparing the nets to go fishing. In the distance, a *dhow* sails out to sea, a timeless sight as the sail ripples, then fills with the Indian Ocean wind.

IMAGES • OF
ZANZIBAR

KHOJA HAJI NASSER NURMAHOMED CHARITABLE

ZANZIBAR
quality
room
air
conditioners

YENU,

OPEN

ANZIBAR TOW
WAPANDAJ
WANAOMBWA

BASKELI
AENDESHE
OLE

MULTICONE
ENTERPRISE
KUMBUKUMBU
BOB MARLEY
J'TANO 11 MEI
STAREHE
THE GALLERY
ZANZIBAR.

JVC

ZAKARI
STORE.
P.O.BOX 76. TEL. 30098. ZANZI

SMZ

HUU NI MJI WETU
KUUWEKA SAFI NI
JUKUMU LETU
ZANZIBAR

ZAINA Mambo
JINI makengel
e.

McGILL

سلطنة عمان
PUMA
IOWA

UNIVERSAL STADIUM

ENCE CAMP

INDEX • TO • THE PHOTOGRAPHS

(Left) An aerial view of the triangular peninsula of the Stone Town in Unguja.

(Left) The Stone Town has more than 500 beautifully carved wooden doors; those with a square frame are classed as Arab while Indian doors have an arched top.

(Left) A lateen-sailed dhow arriving laden with cargo from the mainland.(Right) Stately, crenellated buildings line the waterfront of the Stone Town.

(Left) A woman wearing a colourful *khanga*, with the brass bosses on a door in the background. (Right) Detail of the elaborate floral carving on a door.

(Top left) The Floating Restaurant at Forodhani, where children practice their diving skills at high tide. (Bottom left) The House of Wonders, built by Sultan Seyyid Barghash in 1883. (Right) The beach at Forodhani, with Tembo Hotel in the foreground.

(Left) Looking through an open doorway into a spacious courtyard in the Stone Town. (Right) A papaya tree reclaims a ruined building for nature.

(Left) An intricately carved wooden balcony with the spire of the Anglican Cathedral in the background.
(Right) The Nasur Nurmohamed Dispensary, presented to the Ismaili community by Sir Tharia Thopan. It has been renovated by the Aga Khan Foundation.

(Left) Colourful windows and doors in the Stone Town. Semi-circular windows are typical of Indian houses. Electricity and telephone wires form webs across the street.

(Left) A sign in the Stone Town: 'Cyclists, please ride slowly'. Bicycle bells can be heard jingling around every corner of the town as a warning to pedestrians.

(Left) An Indian woman preparing *bhajias*, made of ground beans mixed with a pinch of chilli and ginger then fried in oil, usually served with a coconut chutney. (Top right) A woman wearing a traditional, black *bui bui*. (Bottom right) Leaving the market.

(Left) *Rikwama* carts are widely used to transport goods through the narrow streets of the town. (Right) Children play with abandoned tyres, keeping them turning with sticks while running alongside.

(Left) The market area bustles with activity in the mornings - you can buy everything from coconuts to grapes. People bring fruit, vegetables and spices from the countryside on local buses or bicycles laden with baskets.

(Left) A man walking in Mkunazini, in the heart of the Stone Town. (Right) Playing with the metal ring from old bicycle tyres is another popular children's game.

(Left) A patchwork of corrugated iron roofs in Ng'ambo, on the outskirts of Zanzibar Town. The houses usually consist of single storey buildings.

(Left) Children studying at a school. (Right) A girl veiled with a *khanga* studying the Koran. Girls begin to cover their heads in public at puberty.

(Left) The streets of the Stone Town are often flooded during the rainy seasons. The *baraza* offers some shelter for those who have time to wait for the deluge to ease.

(Top left) The clock tower of the House of Wonders formerly showed the time measured from sunrise to sunset. (Bottom left) The Courts of Law in the Stone Town. (Right) Beit el-Amani or the Peace Memorial Museum, opened in 1925.

(Left) Children gambling at the Idd celebration, one of the many types of game on offer. (Right) Fishermen playing *bao* on the beach at Mkokotoni, in north-west Unguja. Variations of the game are found throughout Africa.

(Left) A colourful, old building in the market area of Chake Chake, Pemba. (Right) The Customs House in Chake Chake, Pemba.

(Top left) St John's Church, Mbweni built in 1882. A colony for freed slaves was established in the area. (Bottom left) The ruins of Marahubi Palace built by Sultan Barghash for his harem. (Right) Ruins of a stone-built mosque on Tumbatu, an island to the north-west of Unguja.

(Left) A *beni* musician performing in the Idd el-Fitr celebration. (Top right) Preparing for *msewe*, a dance originally from Pemba in which small, woven bags filled with seeds are worn on the legs. (Bottom right) Outside the musicians' tent at the Idd el-Fitr ground.

(Left) An aerial view of a farm surrounded by coconut trees. (Right) A woman carrying coconut wood, an important source of fuel for cooking in villages.

(Left) Kirumbizi, a ritual dance before *mchezo wa ngombe*, the Pemban variation of a bull-fight.

(Left) Bicycles are a useful form of transport for everything from furniture to chickens. (Right) Jozani, a remnant of primeval forest on Unguja, the home of the rare Red Colobus monkey.

(Left) People travelling back to Tumbatu island after visiting the market at Mkokotoni.

(Left) Drying grated coconut which is then used in cooking or to extract oil.

(Top left) A woman weaving *ukindu*, or date palm fronds, imported to Zanzibar and made into mats, baskets and food covers. (Bottom left) Grating a coconut using an *mbuzi*. (Right) The tough coconut shell is split after soaking it in water.

(Left) Women drawing water from a well at Matemwe, a village on the north-east coast of Unguja.

(Left) A man weaving *makuti*, a traditional roofing material made of palm fronds. (Right) *Makuti* is often used to make a fenced courtyard behind local houses, containing the kitchen and bathroom areas.

(Left) Women wearing *khangas*, brightly coloured cotton cloths sold in pairs, usually with a saying in Kiswahili written along the lower border.

(Left) The clove buds are picked before they open, then separated from the stem and spread out to dry on mats in the sun for four to six days.

(Left) Traditional versus modern dress styles seen during the Idd el-Fitr celebration at the end of Ramadhan. Women are usually given a new set of *khangas* as a present at this time.

(Left) Taking the outer husk off a coconut by impaling it on a metal spike called *kifulio*. (Right) Climbing a tree to cut coconuts; men often sing at the top of their voices to warn anyone walking down below.

(Left) Mending a *jarife* net, used to catch larger fish such as tuna and sailfish. (Right) Fishing nets on Nungwi beach, ready to be loaded onto dhows for fishing. The village is situated at the northernmost tip of Unguja island and is famous for the large dhows built there.

(Left) Coconut husks are buried in the sand below the tide line for about three months, then beaten with sticks to obtain strands of fibre which can be made into rope.

(Left) Children punting in the shallows at Bwejuu on the east coast of Unguja.

(Left) A woman harvesting seaweed which is grown on strings suspended between wooden stakes. (Right) Returning to shore with a bag full of seaweed. It will be dried before being exported.

(Left) Scorching a boat to remove worms and other growth from the hull. (Right) A fisherman pulling his *ngalawa* ashore, a fishing boat with double outriggers.

(Left) An aerial view of seaweed plots on the reef flats of the east coast of Unguja. (Right) The carrageenan which is extracted from seaweed is used in products as diverse as chocolate and toothpaste.

(Left) Fishermen at Kiwengwa on Unguja's east coast; the octopus are usually caught using hand spears.

(Left) Boys taking their catch of rays home at Uroa, a beautiful white beach on the east coast of Unguja. (Right) Dragging nets through the water is a popular method of fishing in shallow areas inside the reef.

(Left) Mangapwani, 'the Arab beach'. The idyllic stretch of white sand which supports a traditional fishing community is increasingly visited by tourists. This area has secluded coves which were used to smuggle slaves.

(Left) Hauling up the sail in preparation for a dhow race. This was traditionally held off Forodhani in the Stone Town and the custom has recently been revived.

(Left) Kizimkazi beach in the south of Unguja. A school of dolphins can frequently be seen just off the coast. Kizimkazi is famous for the Kufic inscription in a mosque which dates from 1107 AD.

(Left) Boats hauled up on the beach at Changuu or Prison Island, a popular place for swimming and snorkelling in the crystal clear waters just off Zanzibar Town.

(Left) A sand bank is a popular diving site to view the myriad shades of coral and variety of colourful fish. (Right) Bawe Island, formerly the site of a British army camp, where the Eastern Telegraph Company landed their cable.

(Left) A giant tortoise on Prison Island. They were originally brought from the Seychelles. (Right) An aerial view of dhows off a fishing village at Mazizini, an area to the south of Zanzibar Town.

(Left) Sunrise at Bwejuu on the east coast of Unguja.